Cecilia McDowall

Good News from New England

for SSATB and solo violin

vocal score

OXFORD

UNIVERSITY PRESS

OXFORD
UNIVERSITY PRESS

Great Clarendon Street, Oxford OX2 6DP,
United Kingdom

Oxford University Press is a department of the University of Oxford.
It furthers the University's objective of excellence in research, scholarship,
and education by publishing worldwide. Oxford is a registered trade mark of
Oxford University Press in the UK and in certain other countries

First published 2023

Impression: 1

ISBN 978-0-19-354055-2

Music origination by Anna Williams
Text origination by Katie Johnston

Printed in Great Britain on acid-free paper by
Halstan & Co. Ltd, Amersham, Bucks.

Contents

Composer's note   iv

Texts   v

1. An Unexpected Shore   1

2. Ghost of a Feather   13

3. Thanksgiving   23

Duration: 15 minutes

The solo violin part is available separately as a digital download (ISBN 978–0–19–356698–9).

Composer's note

Good News from New England was commissioned by Geoffrey Smeed for City Chamber Choir in London and its founder and conductor, Stephen Jones. The work is scored for mixed voices with solo violin and draws its title from Edward Winslow's chronicles of 1624, *Good Newes from New England*, in which he describes the early experiences of the *Mayflower* Pilgrims' arrival and settlement in the New World.

'An Unexpected Shore' takes its text from the journal of the Puritan Separatist William Bradford, *Of Plymouth Plantation*. Bradford was chosen to be governor of Plymouth Colony in 1621 and gives a telling account of the arrival of the Pilgrims in a new land after their long and perilous journey. These resilient non-conformist Pilgrims were inspired by a 'sense of earthly grandeur and divine purpose' and the opening movement charts their voyage from one shore to another by gradually descending from A major, through A♭ major, to G major, perhaps bringing a sense of establishing a new community in this harsh landscape.

'Ghost of a Feather' is fashioned from two very different texts, 400 years apart, on the same poignant matter: the death of William Bradford's wife. John Greening's subtle yet powerful poem describes how Bradford's wife fell overboard into a calm sea in the harbour, in December 1620, while her husband was ashore. Conversely, there is something resolute, in the face of catastrophe, in Bradford's own poem, written after his wife Dorothy's tragic death. In setting the Bradford text I adopted a semi-*Bay Psalm Book* idiom, with its plain homophonic style, introducing occasional dissonance to intensify the anguish. In contrast to this, the opening and closing sections of this movement might seem more folk-like, with a violin accompaniment which perhaps reflects the known Celtic influence on fiddle playing in New England at the time. 'Cole's Hill', the title of John Greening's poem, refers to the first burial ground of the Pilgrims in Plymouth.

The third movement brings perhaps a sense of release and joyfulness in thanksgiving. The violin solo is in playful dialogue with the dance-like vocal lines. These words are taken from Winslow's Thanksgiving letter of 1621, written to a friend in England. A year after the *Mayflower* Pilgrims settled in Plymouth, they had much to celebrate. The following section reprises material from the opening movement, which in turn leads to Henry Ainsworth's version of 'The Old Hundredth', which was sung on the *Mayflower* and subsequently in the Plymouth Colony. The audience is encouraged to participate in singing this hymn.

This note may be reproduced as required for programme notes.

The first movement, 'An Unexpected Shore', has been recorded by The Sixteen, conducted by Harry Christophers, on the CD *An Old Belief* (COR16189).

Texts

These texts and melody may be reproduced as required for programme notes and to allow audience participation in the final movement during a performance of *Good News from New England*.

1. An Unexpected Shore

And lo! The winds did blow us ever to the North; so that we that crossed the Seas to seek the Lord's right worship and the Gospell's sweet simplicitie, did now espy an unexpected shore; yet still resolv'd in our extremitie to make it ours, by Compact, orderly and free.

And here is to be noted a spetiall providence of God, and a great mercie. For we did take a better view, and soon resolv'd where to pitch our dwelling; our first house to raise for common use.

William Bradford (1590–1657),
freely adapted and abridged by Nicholas Dakin

2. Ghost of a Feather

A single cry from the ghost of a feather.
A solitary goodwife drops into the bay.
One burial, then another, then another.
The first house on Christmas Day.

'Cole's Hill' by John Greening (b. 1954). © John Greening. Used by permission.

Faint not, poor soul, in God still trust;
Fear not the things thou suffer must;
For, whom he loves he doth chastise,
And then all tears wipes from their eyes.

William Bradford (on the death of his wife, who fell overboard and drowned, aged 23)

3. Thanksgiving

After the famines of the first winter, our harvest now being gotten in, we did after a special manner rejoice and give thanks together, many of the Indians coming in amongst us we entertained and feasted. And although it was not so plentiful again, yet by the goodness of our God, we were so far from want, that we often wished you partakers of our plenty.

Edward Winslow (1595–1655)
Thanksgiving letter, December 1621,
freely adapted and abridged by Nicholas Dakin

For mee a table thou hast spread,
In presence of my foes:
Thou dost annoynt my head with oyle,
My cup it over-flowes.
And in the Lord's house I shall dwell
So long as dayes shall bee.

From Psalm 23, Bay Psalm Book *(1640)*

'The Old Hundredth'

Showt to Jehovah, al the earth,
Serv ye Jehovah with gladnes:
before him come with singing merth.
Know, that Jehovah he God is.

It's he that made us, and not we:
his folk, and sheep of his feeding.
O with confession enter ye his gates,
his courtyards with praising:

Confess to him, bless his name.
Because Jehovah he good is:
his mercy ever is the same
and his faith, unto al ages. Amen.

Henry Ainsworth (1571–1622)*, The Book of Psalmes: Englished both in Prose and Metre (1612)

* Henry Ainsworth, English Congregationalist, wrote the psalter that was used on the *Mayflower* and at Plymouth, in modern-day Massachusetts, by the Pilgrims. Later, the first book published in America would be another psalter, the *Bay Psalm Book*, but when the Pilgrims first sang psalms in the New World, the lines came from the Ainsworth psalter, titled *The Book of Psalmes: Englished both in Prose and Metre with Annotations.*

Commissioned by Geoffrey Smeed for City Chamber Choir and its founder and conductor, Stephen Jones

Good News from New England

CECILIA McDOWALL

1. An Unexpected Shore

William Bradford (1590–1657),
freely adapted and abridged by Nicholas Dakin

Printed in Great Britain

OXFORD UNIVERSITY PRESS, MUSIC DEPARTMENT, GREAT CLARENDON STREET, OXFORD OX2 6DP

4

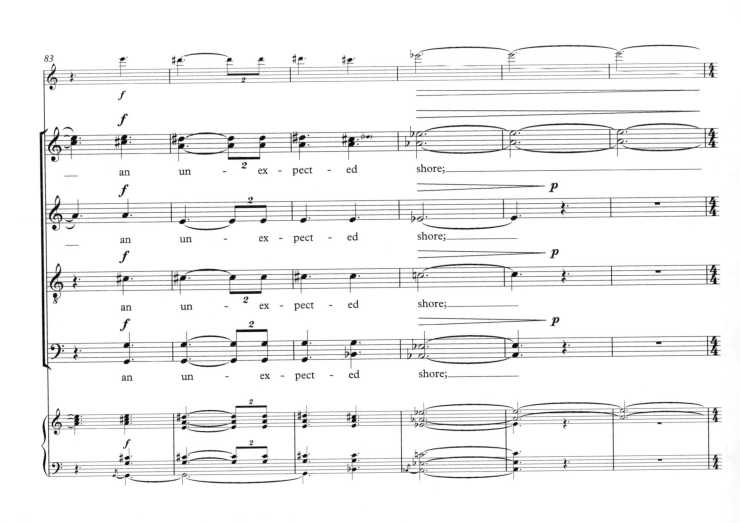

12

2. Ghost of a Feather

John Greening (b. 1954)
William Bradford (1590–1657)

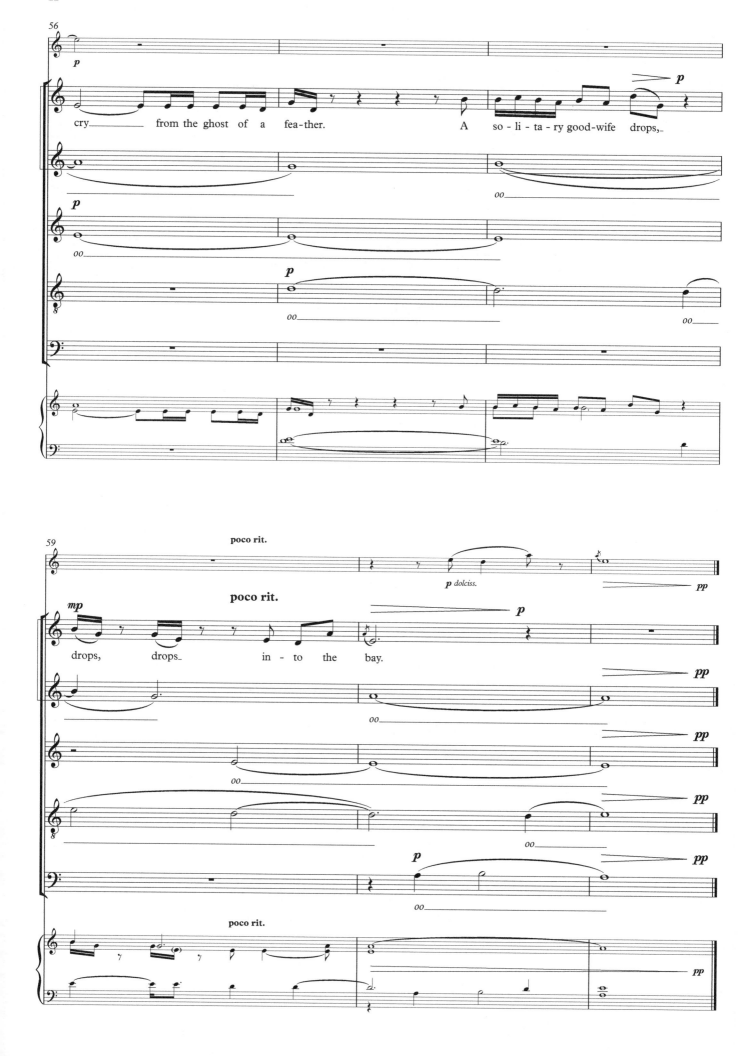

3. Thanksgiving

Edward Winslow (1595–1655),
   freely adapted and abridged by Nicholas Dakin

-mongst us. ah

coming in a - mongst us we en - ter - tained and feast - ed.

coming in a - mongst us we en - ter - tained and feast - ed.

ah

And al - though, and al - though,

And al - though, and al - though,

And al - though, and al - though,

And al - though, and al - though,

al - though it was not so plen - ti - ful a - gain,_____

al - though it was not so plen - ti - ful a - gain,_____ yet_____

al - though it was not so plen - ti - ful a - gain,_____

al - though it was not so plen - ti - ful a - gain,_____ yet_____

God,_____ our God,_____

by the good - ness of__ our__ God,_____ our God,_____

God,_____ our God,_____

by the good - ness of__ our__ God,_____ our God,_____

*Text from Psalm 23, *Bay Psalm Book* (1640)

* 'The Old Hundredth', words and melody from Henry Ainsworth (1571–1622), *The Book of Psalmes: Englished both in Prose and Metre* (1612)